Subtraction Action

Written and illustrated By
Loreen Leedy

Holiday House • New York

For my niece Anna Katherine Leedy

The author would like to thank Professor Donna R. Strand
From the School of Education, Baruch College,
City University of New York, for her assistance.

Printed and bound in October 2017 at Toppan Leefung, DongGuan City, China.
7 9 11 12 10 8
Library of Congress Cataloging-in-Publication Data
Leedy, Loreen.
Subtraction action / by Loreen Leedy.–1st ed.
p. cm.
Summary: introduces subtraction through the activities of animal students at a school fair.
Includes problems for the reader to solve.
ISBN-13: 978-0-8234-1454-3 (hardcover)
ISBN-13: 978-0-8234-1764-3 (paperback)
1. Subtraction—Juvenile literature. [1. Subtraction.] I. Title
QA115.L447 1999
513.2′12-dc21   99-049803
Loreen Leedy's website is www.loreenleedy.com

Our Subtraction Stories

4 - 3 by Sadie

I had four pencils.
The pencil sharpener ate three of them.
I have one pencil left.
4 - 3 = 1

8 – 8 by Otto

My mom baked eight cookies.
I ate all of them.
There were zero cookies left.
8 – 8 = 0

12 – 7 by Fay

Our team scored twelve points.
Their team scored seven points.
We won by five points!
12 – 7 = 5

CONTENTS

9 - 7 by Tally

I had nine old toys.
I sold seven at a garage sale.
I had two toys left.
9 - 7 = 2

10 - 6 by Ginger

I grew ten big tomatoes.
I gave six of them away.
I had four tomatoes left.
10 - 6 = 4

Miss Prime showed her class a sign, a book, and a piece of paper.

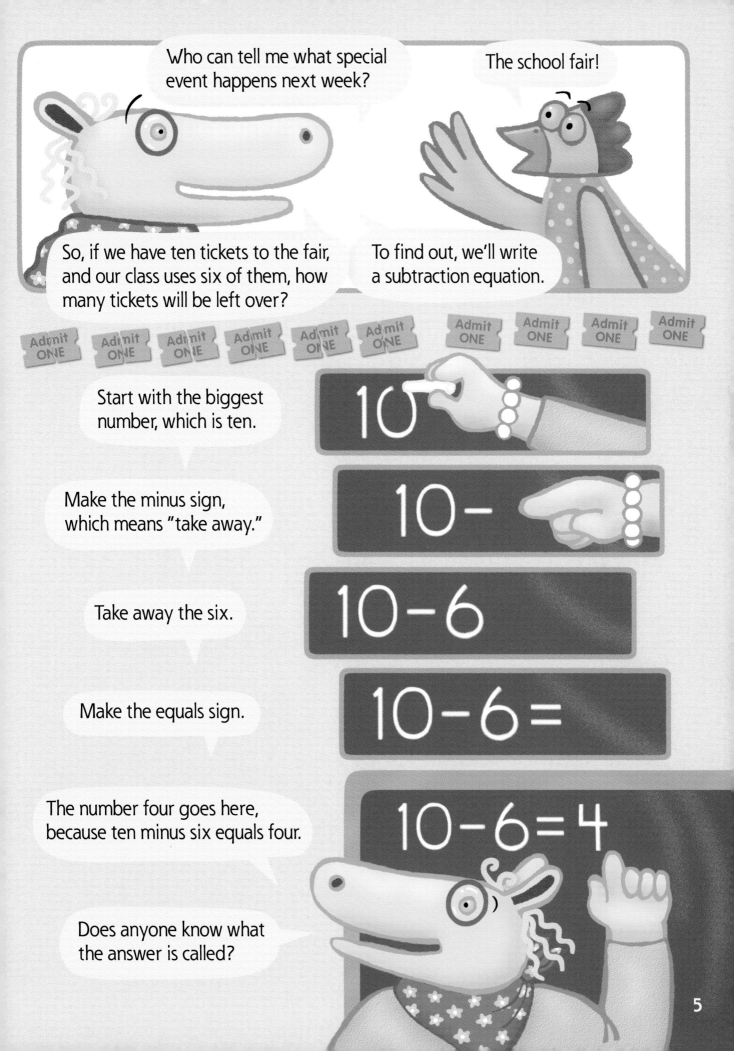

Who can tell me what special event happens next week?

The school fair!

So, if we have ten tickets to the fair, and our class uses six of them, how many tickets will be left over?

To find out, we'll write a subtraction equation.

Start with the biggest number, which is ten.

10

Make the minus sign, which means "take away."

10-

Take away the six.

10-6

Make the equals sign.

10-6=

The number four goes here, because ten minus six equals four.

10-6=4

Does anyone know what the answer is called?

Fair Is Fair

Ginger and Sadie waited to get their faces painted at the school fair.

What is the missing number?

$$7 - \_\_ = 2 \qquad \_\_ - 4 = 1$$

Answers: page 32

LeSS IS LeSS

$$10 - 2 - 3 = 5$$

TAKE SOME TIME OFF

A popular event at the school fair was the obstacle course.

START

FINISH

16

How much time did Fay subtract from the original school record? From Chester's time? Answers: page 32

MinuS MaGiC

Miss Prime put on a magic show at the school fair.

I'll just say the magic words: **minus two!**

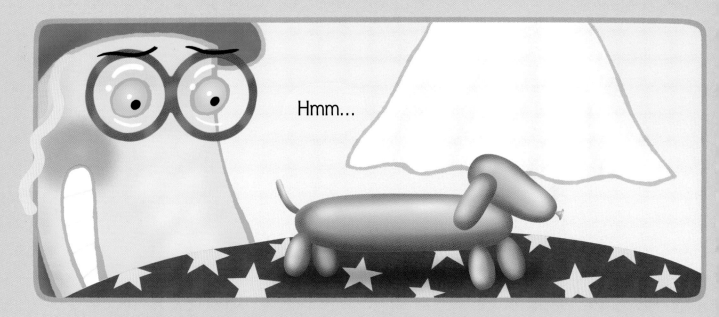

Going, Going, Gone

Tally and Otto were selling snacks at the fair.

Hey, Tally, how much will you pay me to eat your popcorn?

Popcorn

Candy Apples

Do we get to eat the leftovers?

$1.00 $1.00

Tally had ten bags of popcorn and sold six.
Otto had eight candy apples and sold three.
Who had the least left over? Answer: page 32

NOThinG to LOSE

Sadie was determined to win a big, fuzzy stuffed bear.

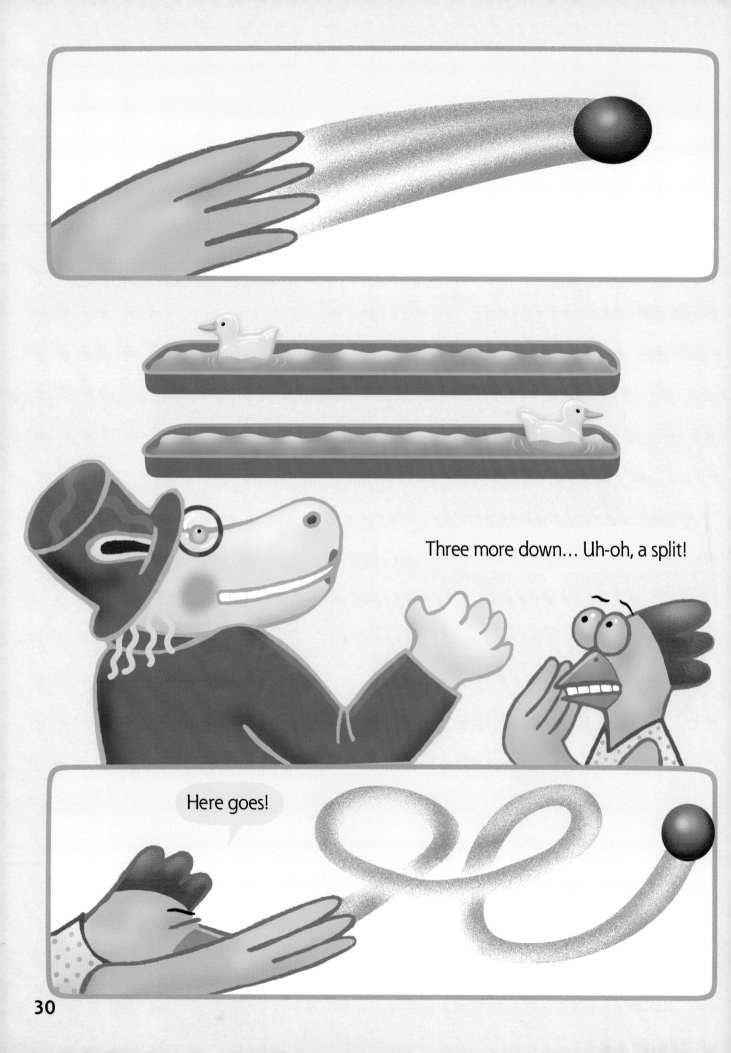

Three more down… Uh-oh, a split!

Here goes!

How can you write Sadie's score as a subtraction equation?

Answer: page 32

Answers

page 6: The equation should read $9-6=3$ or $9-3=6$.

page 9: The missing number is five.
$7-\underline{5}=2$ $\underline{5}-4=1$

page 13: The difference between ten and five is five. $10-5=5$

page 19: Fay subtracted five seconds from the original time. $30-25=5$
Fay subtracted one second from Chester's time. $26-25=1$

page 24: I am the number nine. $20-11=9$

page 28: Tally had the least left over, because $10-6=4$ bags of popcorn and $8-3=5$ candy apples.

page 31: Sadie's score: $10-5-3-2=0$